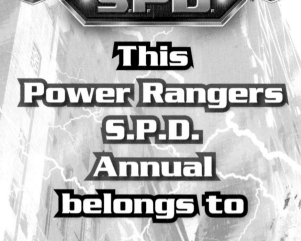

Power Rangers S.P.D.

This
Power Rangers
S.P.D.
Annual
belongs to

Daniel Kemp

spd online
www.jetix.co.uk/spd

downloads

games

character info

pick a ranger

watch power rangers every day
Only on Jetix

POWER RANGERS
S.P.D.
ANNUAL 2007

Edited by Jo Strange   Designed by Colin Treanor

EGMONT
We bring stories to life

First published in Great Britain in 2006 by Egmont UK Limited
239 Kensington High Street, London W8 6SA
ISBN 978 1 4052 2604 2
ISBN 1 4052 2604 8
10 9 8 7 6 5 4 3 2 1
Printed in Italy

JETIX™
www.jetix.co.uk

POWER RANGERS S.P.D.

Welcome to your Power Rangers S.P.D. Annual!

It's the year 2025 and humans are living alongside aliens from distant planets. Commander Cruger, head of the S.P.D. Academy, has the job of training the very latest team of Power Rangers. As well as keeping the peace in Newtech City, these highly skilled recruits have a bigger mission: to protect the Earth from the evil Emperor Gruumm!

Inside, get ready to find out all there is to know about the S.P.D. Power Rangers. There are brilliant stories, plus profiles, power-packed puzzles and more. Are you ready to put your S.P.D. skills to the test?

CONTENTS

CRUGER'S MEMO

To: SUPREME COMMANDER
FOWLER BIRDIE,
GALAXY COMMAND

From: COMMANDER
ANUBIS CRUGER,
DELTA BASE, EARTH

Supreme Commander,
    Your last memo raised doubts as to whether Space Patrol Delta's B-Squad was prepared for the tough battle that lies ahead.

I agree.
However, I think we disagree on the nature of that battle. Let me explain by going through some details about this unique unit of Power Rangers.

B-Squad was formed as a back-up to S.P.D.'s A-Squad. When the Troobian Forces of Emperor Gruumm targeted Earth, A-Squad was sent to meet the threat.

We await news of A-Squad's latest mission to the Helix Nebula. The job of protecting Earth, meanwhile, has passed to B-Squad.

9

B-Squad is made up of three highly trained S.P.D. Academy graduates and two gifted special recruits. These special recruits are Jack Landors, the Red Ranger, and Elizabeth 'Z' Delgado, the Yellow Ranger.

Their unusual lifestyles as street-smart "Robin Hoods" – giving food and clothing to the poor – coupled with their extraordinary powers, brought them to my attention.

Jack's ability to pass through solid objects and Z's power to create duplicates of herself would assist the three Academy graduates.

Sky Tate, the Blue Ranger, Bridge Carson, the Green Ranger and Sydney Drew, the Pink Ranger, have special powers themselves.

Sky can create force-fields; Bridge has psychic abilities and Syd's hands can turn into any element she touches. Combining the five into a single team was common sense.

To add to those powers and the superb hand-to-hand fighting skills each member has, B-Squad has access to our very latest technology.

The Delta Morphers they carry allow them to morph into Ranger form and to communicate with each other.

The morphers also act as "Judgement Scanners". In this mode, they give quick read-outs on the guilt or innocence of suspects. A Judgement is never wrong.

Jack carries Delta Blasters and the others have Deltamax Strikers. These weapons can digitally capture the guilty, sealing them on to a Containment Card.

Most enemies, like Emperor Gruumm's Krybot foot-soldiers or their Bluehead commanders, can be dealt with using these weapons.

For larger villains, B-Squad has the Robotic Interactive Canine at its disposal. The R.I.C. resembles an Earth creature called a dog – indeed, I am sometimes compared to the same creature myself!

R.I.C is a multi-function robot that aids the Rangers in tracking and capturing criminals. It can transform into the Canine Cannon to boost B-Squad's firepower.

Operating out of Delta Base, the Rangers have been given the Delta Runners. These are fast emergency vehicles which, using the latest technology, combine to form the Delta Squad Megazord.

This giant robot has the strength and weaponry to deal with the most dangerous and powerful fighting machines that Gruumm has so far used in his quest to conquer Earth.

Gruumm's evil schemes to destroy this planet mean he is sure to find many deadly alien criminals for his army in the future. To combat their threat, we have more hi-tech improvements planned. I believe B-Squad will have the hardware it needs to meet the challenge, however it is not this battle that worries me most ...

My biggest fear is the battle B-Squad faces with itself. For Power Rangers, the Red Ranger is the leader – the best of the best. Jack holds this position, despite being an outsider.

Jack must give orders to the three S.P.D. Academy graduates, even though they have spent years in training. Sky, the Blue Ranger, finds this very difficult.

Sky's father was once a Red Power Ranger and Sky feels he should have the same rank. Sky and Jack have already clashed at times. While they work out their differences, more rows are possible in the future.

This is the real battleground. Can B-Squad come to terms with its own talent? Can the five Rangers unlock their true potential as a team? As they face the dangers ahead, that battle has only just begun – and its outcome is uncertain.

RED

Jack, the Red S.P.D. Ranger, grew up on the streets of Newtech City, where he spent his time trying to help those less fortunate than himself. His desire to help others impressed Commander Cruger, as did his special powers. When Jack first joined the S.P.D. Academy, he found it hard to follow rules. Jack likes to do things his own way!

FULL NAME:
Jack Landors

BRAINS	8

TOP GEAR:
Delta Morpher, Patrol Cycle

STRENGTH	10

WEAPONS:
Delta Blasters

SKILL	9

S.P.D. RANGER

S.P.D-ARMS
R-01-2

ZORD:
Delta Runner 1
POWER 8

SPECIAL SKILL:
Martial arts
COOLNESS 9

POWERS:
Jack has the ability to pass through solid objects
GOODNESS 10

DID YOU KNOW?
Jack's Delta Blasters combine to form the Delta Blasters Combo.

BLUE

Sky, the Blue Ranger, likes to do everything by the book. Following tough training at the S.P.D. Academy, Sky has developed expert fighting skills and a talent for reporting on criminals. At first he felt angry that Jack was chosen to be the Red Ranger instead of him. However, having seen Jack's strong leadership skills, he is learning to accept his role as second in command.

FULL NAME:
Schuyler 'Sky' Tate

BRAINS	9

TOP GEAR:
Delta Morpher, Patrol Cycle

STRENGTH	8

WEAPONS:
Deltamax Striker

SKILL	9

S.P.D. RANGER

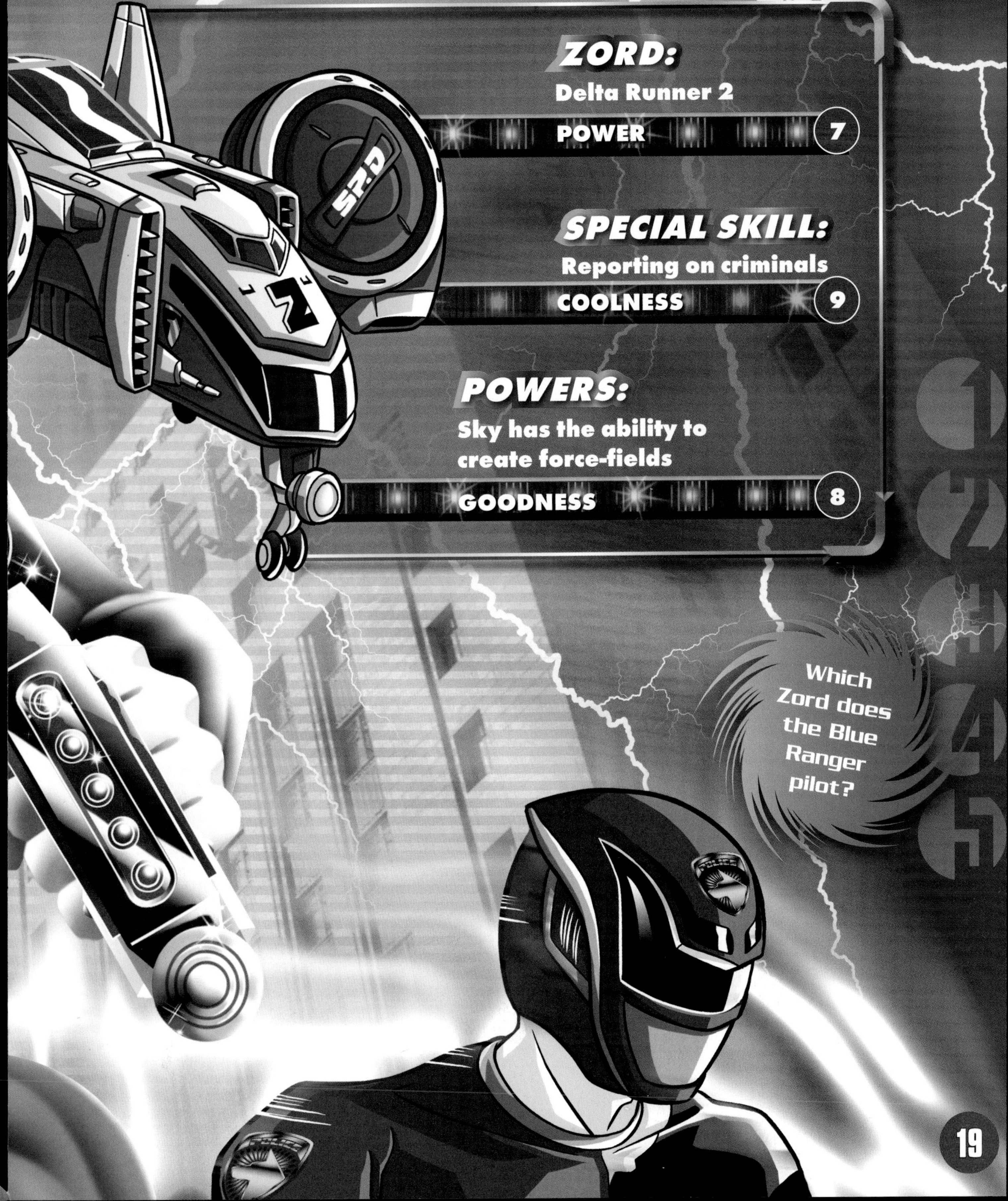

ZORD:
Delta Runner 2
POWER 7

SPECIAL SKILL:
Reporting on criminals
COOLNESS 9

POWERS:
Sky has the ability to create force-fields
GOODNESS 8

Which Zord does the Blue Ranger pilot?

GREEN

Bridge, the Green Ranger, is often seen as a bit of scatterbrain. In fact, he is very intelligent and knows all about mechanics. This, along with his incredible psychic-tracking powers, makes him an important member of the S.P.D. team.

FULL NAME:

Bridge Carson

BRAINS　　　10

TOP GEAR:

Delta Morpher, Patrol Cycle

STRENGTH　　8

WEAPONS:

Deltamax Striker

SKILL　　8

S.P.D. RANGER

ZORD:
Delta Runner 3

POWER 9

SPECIAL SKILL:
Mechanics

COOLNESS 9

POWERS:
Bridge can track evil using psychic powers

GOODNESS 10

DID YOU KNOW?
Bridge credits his intelligence to his habit of standing on his head!

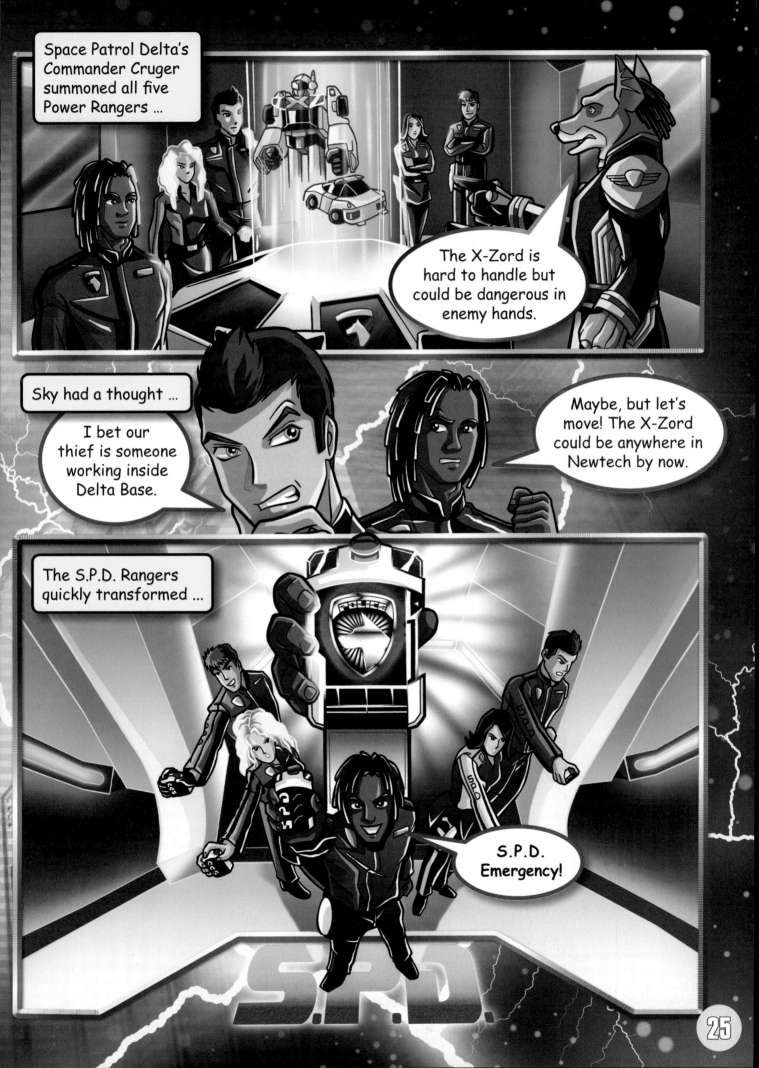

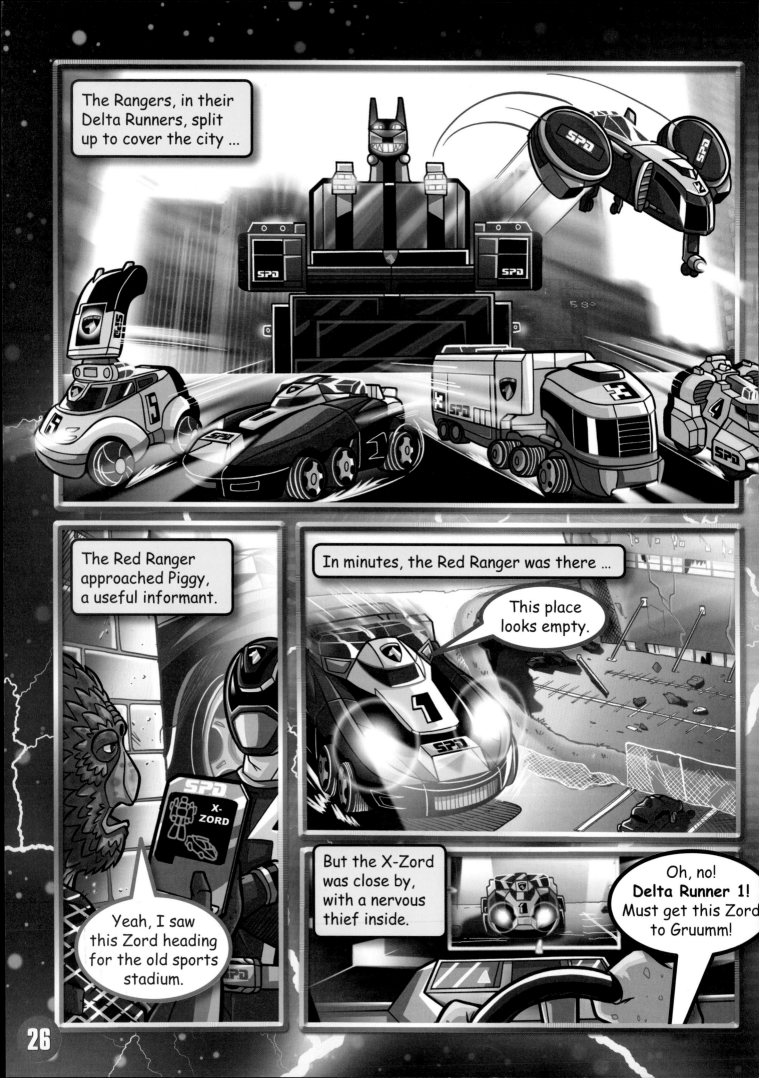

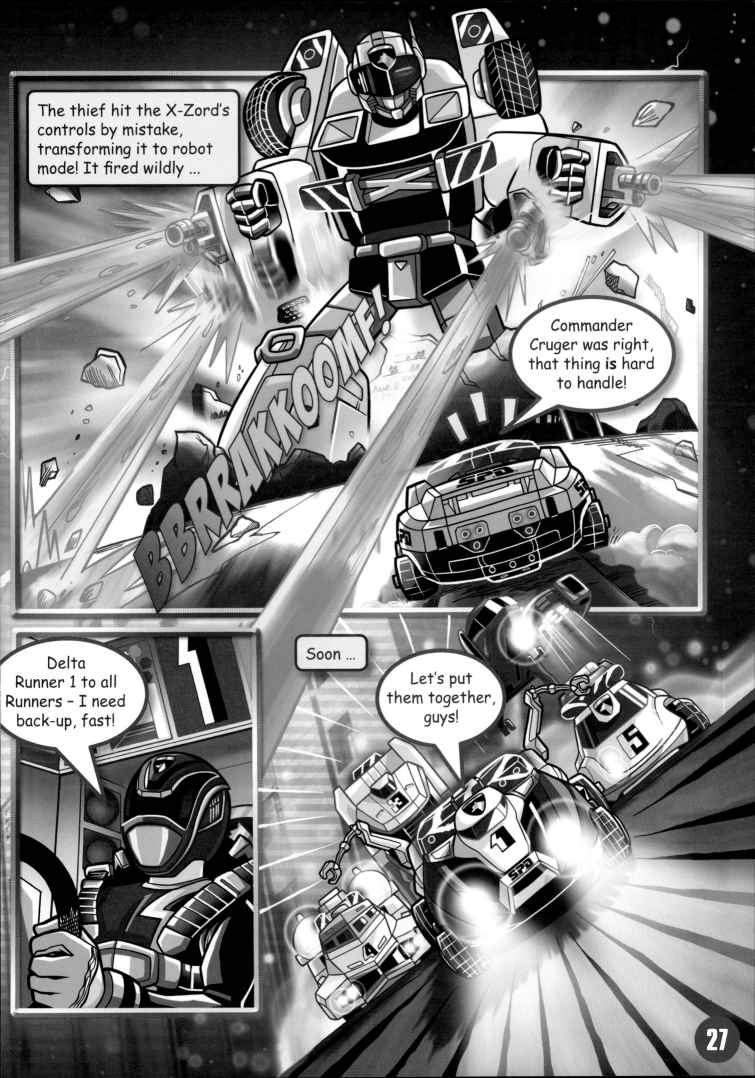

PROFILE

Emperor Gruumm is the leader of the Troobian Empire, a planet-conquering alien force. Not happy with destroying Commander Cruger's home planet of Sirius, evil Gruumm has now set his sights on Earth!

FULL NAME:

Emperor Gruumm

BRAINS   9

TOP GEAR:

Evil Cycle

STRENGTH   5

ROBOTIC ARMY:

Krybots

SKILL   7

EMPEROR GRUUMM

HIDE-OUT:
Terror Spacecraft

POWER — 8

ASSISTANTS:
Mora, Blueheads

EVILNESS — 10

POWERS:
Gruumm can pick things up with his mind and crush them

GOODNESS — 0

DID YOU KNOW?
Commander Cruger cut off Emperor Gruumm's right horn during battle.

DELTA MATCH

The little pictures all appear in the large Delta Runners above. How quickly can you spot them?

a

b

c

d

e

f

g

Answers on page 68.

TARGET STRIKE

See if you can blast six red targets as you power your way through this maze.

START

FINISH

S.P.D. PROFILE

PINK

Syd, the Pink Ranger, is from a rich family. She always looks good but don't be fooled – this cadet can hold her own in any battle. Although she can seem spoiled, Syd values her friendships and enjoys helping her team-mates to become better Rangers.

FULL NAME:
Sydney 'Syd' Drew

BRAINS	8

TOP GEAR:
Delta Morpher, Delta Cruiser

STRENGTH	7

WEAPONS:
Deltamax Striker

SKILL	7

S.P.D. RANGER

What is Syd's special skill?

ZORD:

Delta Runner 5

POWER — 8

SPECIAL SKILL:

Surveillance Expert

COOLNESS — 9

POWERS:

Syd is able to turn her hands into any element she touches

GOODNESS — 9

S.P.D.

Bridge, Jack and Sky need some bright colours to power them into action!

BRIDGE

GREEN
S.P.D.
RANGER

EMERGENCY!

SKY

BLUE
S.P.D.
RANGER

ACK

RED
S.P.D.
RANGER

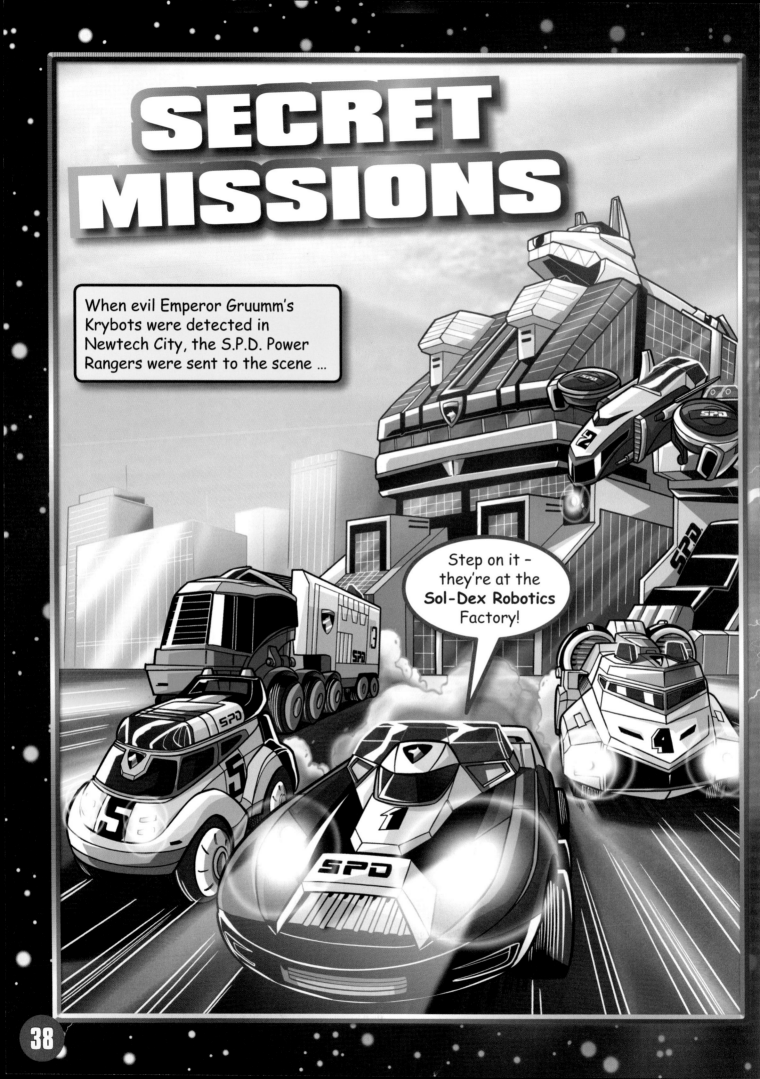

As Bridge checked R.I.C. he suddenly recalled something ...

Earlier, I used my **psychic power** to detect Sol-Dex's aura, but I couldn't find one on that engineer. Watch him, Syd ...

Meanwhile, on his spaceship, Emperor Gruumm was pleased ...

You have done well!

The next day, Syd was in disguise at the factory.

Hmm, there's that engineer, behaving oddly ...

YELLOW

Like Jack, Z, the Yellow Ranger, grew up on the streets. Her aim in life was to help the poor, even if that meant stealing from the rich. All Z wanted was to be part of something better. Since joining the S.P.D. Academy, Z hasn't looked back. She fully understands her mission – to serve and protect the galaxy!

FULL NAME:
Elizabeth 'Z' Delgado

BRAINS 9

TOP GEAR:
Delta Morpher, Delta Cruiser

STRENGTH 7

WEAPONS:
Deltamax Striker

SKILL 6

S.P.D. RANGER

ZORD:

Delta Runner 4

POWER   7

SPECIAL SKILL:

Excellent negotiator

COOLNESS   8

POWERS:

Z is able to make duplicates of herself

GOODNESS   9

Can you point to the Yellow Ranger's Deltamax Striker?

KRYBOT ATTACK

Can you find 10 differences between these two pictures?

Answers on page 68.

SQUAD MEGAZORD

Colour the mighty
Squad Megazord using
the coloured dots
to help you.

Commander Cruger is the leader of the S.P.D. team. When necessary, he morphs into the Shadow Ranger – a wise and experienced fighter. Years ago, Cruger's home planet of Sirius was attacked by Emperor Gruumm. Cruger was the only survivor and ever since, he has sworn to put a stop to Emperor Gruumm's evil plans.

FULL NAME:
Commander Anubis Cruger

BRAINS — 10

TOP GEAR:
Patrol Morpher, Delta Patrol ATV

STRENGTH — 7

WEAPONS:
Shadow Sabre

SKILL — 8

SHADOW S.P.D. RANGER

ZORD:

Delta Command

POWER 9

SPECIAL SKILL:

Strong leadership

COOLNESS 7

POWERS:

The Shadow Ranger has the power of Super Speed

GOODNESS 8

PERSONAL DATA

▽ CODE NAME
SHADOW RANGER

▽ D-ARMS
SHADOW SABER

POLICE

DID YOU KNOW? Commander Cruger is also known as 'Doggie'.

PROFILE

OMEGA

Sam, the Omega Ranger, joined
S.P.D. as a young boy when he was
befriended by the Yellow Ranger.
Fifteen years later, he was sent
back in time to 2025 to help the
S.P.D. team in the battle against
Gruumm. Sam is equipped with
a hi-tech morpher that comes
with superior attack modes.

FULL NAME:

Sam's full name is never revealed

BRAINS 9

TOP GEAR:

Omega Morpher, Uniforce Cycle

STRENGTH 8

WEAPONS:

Sam's Omega Morpher also
acts as his battle weapon

SKILL 10

S.P.D. RANGER

ZORD:

Omegamax Cycle

POWER — 9

SPECIAL SKILL:

Technology expert

COOLNESS — 10

POWERS:

Sam can transport things through teleportation

GOODNESS — 8

DID YOU KNOW?
Sam's parents helped create the S.P.D. Rangers' Morphers.

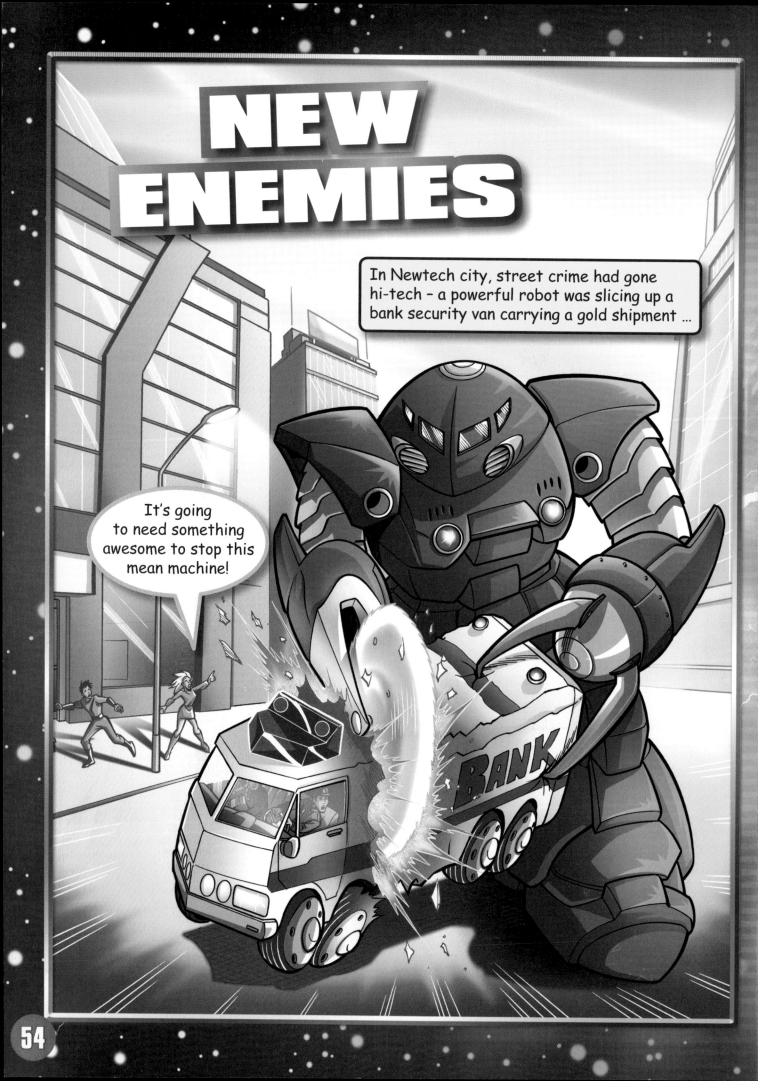

The Green Ranger put his Patrol Cycle lasers to use ...

Z-Z-ZA-BOOOMMFF!

... while the Red Ranger reached for his Delta Blasters.

KA-THAMM!

The third Ro-dog found its target ...

GRRAAAAH!

Aargh!

KA-THAMM!

The Blue Ranger looked doomed, until ...

CATCH A

Follow the Blue Ranger's steps to learn how to catch a criminal – S.P.D. style!

STEP 1

LOCATE THE ENEMY ...

Once you've spotted your criminal, keep yourself out of sight and approach the scene with caution.

STEP 2

MOVE IN ...

Unlock your Containment Cuffs and hold them ready. Come in close behind the criminal but be careful not to make a sound.

CRIMINAL

STEP 3

CAPTURE!

In one move, leap out and surprise the criminal and slam the Cuffs on to their wrists. Now they're ready to be judged!

STEP 4

FINAL JUDGEMENT

Hold your Delta Morpher in Judgement Mode and take a reading. If they're guilty, zap them on to a Containment Card!

RANGER CHALLENGE

Which colour Ranger comes next in each row? Use your brightest pens to complete each sequence.

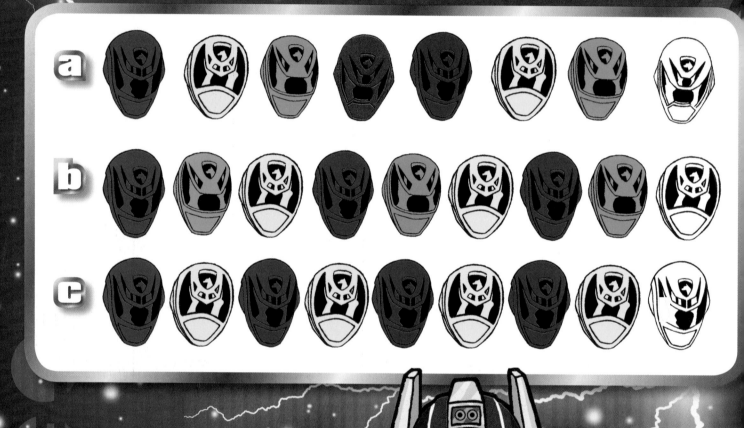

BLAST THE BLUEHEADS!

Look at the page carefully. Close your eyes and, using a pen, try to land a dot on each of the Bluehead Krybot heads!

How many Blueheads did you blast?

**Could you be an S.P.D. Power Ranger?
Try Commander Cruger's quiz to find out! Look back
through the annual to find the answers.**

1 B-Squad was initially formed as a back-up to which S.P.D. squad?
a) C-Squad
b) A-Squad
c) Squad-1

2 Why is Sky jealous of Jack?
a) Jack was chosen to be the Red Ranger
b) Jack's Delta Runner is faster than his
c) Jack is taller than him

3 What is Z's special power?
a) She has psychic abilities
b) She can make duplicates of herself
c) She can pass through solid objects

4 What are Emperor Gruumm's elite soldiers called?
a) Redheads
b) Blackheads
c) Blueheads

5 In the "New Enemies" story, which criminal was working for Broodwing?
a) Ricco Vardman
b) Reko Veltman
c) Richie Vernall

6 Where is the Rangers' Delta Base located?
a) Newtech City
b) Tech Town
c) Delta City

7 What weapon can the Robotic Interactive Canine form?
a) Canine Blaster
b) Canine Striker
c) Canine Cannon

8 Which two Rangers once lived on the streets?
a) Jack and Z
b) Jack and Syd
c) Jack and Sky

Now check the answers on page 68 and add up your score. Are you ready to join the S.P.D. Academy?

Power Rangers S.P.D.

This is to certify that

....

has successfully completed
cadet training at the S.P.D. Academy.
Fill in your Ranger details below:

Power Ranger Name:

....

Age:

....

Special Skill:

....

Ranger Weapon:

....

Well done, Ranger! You are now ready to join the S.P.D. team, to serve and protect the galaxy!

ANSWERS

19 BLUE S.P.D. RANGER

The Blue Ranger pilots
Delta Runner 2.

32 DELTA MATCH

33 TARGET STRIKE

35 PINK S.P.D. RANGER

Syd's special skill is surveillance.

48 KRYBOT ATTACK

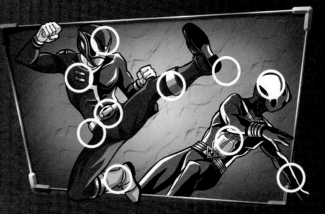

64 RANGER CHALLENGE

66 CRUGER'S QUIZ

For every correct answer,
award yourself one point.

1 – b; 2 – a; 3 – b; 4 – c; 5 – b; 6 – a;
7 – c; 8 – a.

CRUGER'S RATING:
0-2: Hmm, you show potential but
there is still more training to be done.

3-5: Not bad! It's clear you have what
it takes to become an S.P.D. Ranger.

6-8: Are you sure you're not a Ranger
already? The galaxy is in safe hands
with you!